HUNTING WILD HAMSTERS

HUNTING WILD HAMSTERS

JANET E. MURPHY AND MICHAEL R. MURPHY

Janet Murphy, SunFace Design

CONTENTS

Were domestic hamsters too inbred for scientists to use for studying natural behaviors? Domestic hamsters all descended from siblings caught in 1930. Michael R. Murphy's quest to obtain wild hamsters successfully secured 12 live wild hamsters in 1971. The resulting colony of wild hamsters was essential to scientists and led to important new scientific findings.

The trip was of historical significance, not only because it was the first time that wild hamsters were brought back from Syria in the 40 years since the first capture, but also because many of the locations we visited during this expedition have been badly damaged or destroyed in recent years. We took a plethora of beautiful photographs during the excursion.

This account describes the people and places we encountered. We visited historical sites in Syria such as the Krak des Chevaliers crusader castle, ancient Ugarit, a Roman road, Resafsa - the city of cisterns, Hama - the city of water wheels, and Qalaat Simeon - where the saint lived atop a pillar. In Lebanon we visited Baalbek and Jaita Grotto. We explored the Aleppo Citadel and the Aleppo souq - the largest historic covered market in the world. We interacted with important figures, such as archaeologists Khaled al Asaa'd and Oleg Graber and important people in Aleppo such as Dr. Iskander Kassis and Dr. Gieo Orita. I also reflect on being a foreigner and a woman in such circumstances.

CHAPTER 1

The Call of Adventure

24 July 1981 • Vol. 213 • No. 4506 $2.00

SCIENCE

AMERICAN ASSOCIATION FOR THE ADVANCEMENT OF SCIENCE

Hamster on "Science" cover for Murphy's article

We had sixty hamsters in our basement. Not gerbils – they are dark and have long tails. Not guinea pigs – they are nearly the size of a football and have tiny tails. Syrian golden hamsters are larger than a mouse, have especially short stubby tails, and sport a softly shining golden coat with wide white collar and chest and black highlights. Their eyes are black, and their furry ears stand up and are rounded in silhouette. They often sit up on their hind legs like an Easter bunny, their little paws up in readiness to hold a small wood chip for nesting material perhaps.

My husband liked to relate something that occurred after his first talk at a scientific convention. He said, "I was 'informed' by a member of the audience that the hamster was a cross between a rat and a guinea pig, and although there were many doubts expressed, neither I nor any other of those present was confident enough to challenge this absurd hybrid notion." Hamsters are, indeed, a separate species, *Mesocricetus auratus Waterhouse.*

But why would anyone have sixty hamsters at one time? The explanation begins here.

There was a time when we had no hamsters at home at all. But there were hamsters at my husband's laboratory at the Massachusetts Institute of Technology, where he was a graduate student in the Psychology Department, studying the brain and its behavior connections. My husband, Michael Ross Murphy, enjoyed working with the animals and always made sure they had clean cages, sufficient food and water, and nesting material. Each of his animals had a large individual plastic box cage with a sturdy wire or perforated metal lid with hole-punch sized holes. A water bottle was mounted upside-down in the lid and was stoppered with a metal nipple. Water did not come out unless the animal lapped at the nipple.

The animals were housed separately because they are solitary animals and the females are rather aggressive with other hamsters, especially males. Yet they are docile with humans and make good pets. He found that those cute furry creatures displayed interesting behaviors for a psychologist to study. He was especially interested in their mating and territorial behavior, which he showed was highly dependent upon their sense of smell. He discovered that if they could not smell they refused to mate or defend their territory.

Other scientists had discovered that hamsters did not get tooth decay or reject transplanted organs the way humans do. Michael pondered why hamsters were so unusual and he read everything he could find about them and corresponded with other scientists by mail, this being before the days of email.

He learned that all the hamsters kept for pets or in scientific laboratories were descendants of one small family of golden hamsters captured in the wild in April of 1930. A mother hamster and her eleven babies were taken from their little burrow in the hard dry land near Aleppo, Syria, by a Hebrew zoologist named Israel Aharoni, and brought back to his university in Jerusalem. Eventually, four of the siblings, one male and three females, survived, and they became the ancestors of all the Syrian golden hamsters in captivity currently in 1970. Thus, all Syrian golden hamsters in pet stores or research laboratories were descended from those siblings!

Michael hypothesized that inbreeding may be the cause of the animal's unusual characteristics, in which case, it would be useful to compare wild hamsters with the ones in the laboratory. Therefore, he considered the possibility of going to Syria to attempt to capture some wild hamsters. It would be the first live capture of hamsters in 40 years.

He obtained permission and the funds for the trip from the Psychology Department at M.I.T. and the Sloan Foundation. I would go along as an assistant and photographer at our own expense. We were both 25 years old and had very little experience with international travel except for a single five-week exploration on our own of Italy and Greece in May-June of 1970. Could we accomplish the task? No one else had done so in forty years.

There was real risk. A long war between Israel and Syria had just ended and we would be among the first Americans to enter Syria after the war. But we were young, immersed in science and study rather than politics or international affairs, and quite unaware of such risks.

Michael proceeded to make the necessary arrangements. We would need a car and live-capture animal traps, as well as permission to import any animals we might capture. He corresponded with various scientists with possible knowledge of hamsters and especially those working in Syria or teaching at the American University in Beirut, Lebanon.

Before we left Boston, our friends gave us a Bon Voyage party. They even made a cake in the shape of a hamster!

Michael and Janet Murphy at Bon Voyage
party

CHAPTER 2

Michael Ross Murphy

But who was this brash young Ph.D. student who thought he could just bring back some wild hamsters from Syria? A little background information might help.

In this account I refer to my husband as Michael, my personal affectionate preference, although most people called him Mike, or just Murphy. He was six feet tall, had an average build, possessed very dark brown hair and brown eyes with long eyelashes. His sense of humor knew no bounds and he was especially fond of making off-the-cuff puns. He had a couple of friends who enjoyed having spontaneous 'pun battles' with him, each fellow quipping a pun in quick response to the other's on the same topic. This was enormously fun to watch and could inspire another pun to be offered from the friends in attendance. I was not the only one who considered him brilliant.

Michael's mother was divorced and he spent his childhood living with his grandparents on their small ranch near Floresville, south of San Antonio, Texas. Both grandparents were intelligent and well-educated. His mother remarried to a Navy computer specialist. While living with them in Key West, Florida, Michael developed Type 1 diabetes. He never let it limit him and managed the disease so well that doctors were impressed with how little damage it did to his body over the years. Despite being a 'Navy brat' who suffered frequent moves and attended five different high schools, Michael was the Valedictorian at his high school graduation in Vallejo, California.

Michael and I met when we were Freshmen at Occidental College, a highly respected liberal arts school in Los Angeles. I was a fellow math major and the daughter of the Airport Manager in San Diego. Michael changed his major to psychology before his junior year, and I transferred to U.C.L.A. for my last two years. I pursued a double major in math and psychology there because I wanted to be cognizant of Michael's interests while I focused my own interest in the new field of computers.

Michael attended the special M.I.T. program in psychology that took five years, skipping the master's degree and going directly to the Ph.D. He studied neuroanatomy under Dr. Walla Nauta, learning to slice and stain hamster brains to detect their underlying structures. His thesis advisor was Dr. Gerald (Jerry) Schneider, a young professor who was also interested in the brain structures involved in certain natural behaviors.

Michael exhibited leadership skills in his undergraduate and graduate days, while simultaneously delving deeply into his particular areas of study. If he was going to use hamsters in the lab then he wanted to know absolutely everything about hamsters. If hamsters exhibited unusual characteristics, he wanted to know why. To find out, he had to go to Syria, and I was expected to accompany him, of course.

CHAPTER 3

In the Heart of London

On May 6, 1971, we left for London for a brief stop to visit the Natural History section of the British Museum and study the type specimen that was used to define the species of *Mesocricetus auratus Waterhouse*, the Syrian golden hamster. From Heathrow airport we made our foray into London, the famous city that had featured so prominently in our college history classes and English literature studies. We settled into the Embassy Court Hotel in Kensington, and Michael made an appointment at the Natural History Museum to have access to the restricted area containing the specimens defining various animal species.

As we awaited the appointment we sampled London's many sights and sounds. Like intrepid explorers on a daring expedition, we ventured into the heart of London, a metropolis steeped in history and teeming with new experiences for us.

"Look! A double-deck bus!" I exclaimed.

" I want a photo of you in that red telephone box," Michael directed, and I posed cheerfully.

Throughout London we found iconic sights such as Big Ben, which we learned refers to the Great Bell, not the Clock Tower housing it. One of the most prominent symbols of London, the tower is 316 feet (96 meters) tall. We couldn't miss it. We found St. Paul's Cathedral, located at the highest point of the city. We recognized Tower Bridge and Buckingham Palace.

Westminster Abbey and its tombs of important and famous people was one of our most memorable visits. We spent the most time at the far end of the nave where we paid homage to the tombs of renowned scientists, including the revered Isaac Newton.

"Newton invented the Calculus," I noted. I was familiar with his contributions to physics, but I had majored in math.

The Poet's Corner held the gravesite of the literary giant Charles Dickens, whose works have enthralled generations. Of course, we had read *Great Expectations*, *David Copperfield*, and *A Tale of Two Cities*, but I had found his writing style extraordinary and had read several of his other works.

"Here is Tennyson," Michael said, and he quoted a few of Tennyson's lines. He was fond of poetry. I found Geoffrey Chaucer. When we ran across the tomb of someone whose name we recognized, we usually stopped to appreciate that person's importance.

We dined on traditional British food like fish and chips and shepherd's pie, noting that green peas were ubiquitous, and that Indian food was also a good option. In fact, we soon got tired of overcooked peas and sought out Indian or Chinese restaurants. We also dropped in to experience the city's pub life, where we sampled local beers and struck up conversations with friendly locals. We were enchanted by the British accent.

We tried to attend several plays, and managed to attend "Hair", "Girl in My Soup", "Canterbury Tales", and "Sleuth", because London was famous for its theaters, and we could try to go every night. In my estimation "Canterbury Tales" at the Phoenix Theatre was very bawdy, had dreadful music, but interesting costumes. We attended "Sleuth" at the St. Martin's Theatre, enjoying a chocolate sundae during the interval. This production was one we enjoyed thoroughly, and were suitably surprised by the extremely loud gunshots in the play. Our impression of the performance of the contemporary musical "Hair" was good, but we found the audience rather dull.

We attended the House of Lords while it was in session debating a bill about unions. We noticed the Lord High Chancellor in his wig. The men had bowler hats and umbrellas.

We found the Sherlock Holmes pub, and climbed the narrow stairs to the restaurant, where the decor featured items described in the detective story books and even some items once belonging to the author, Arthur Conan Doyle, himself. It felt very British, very Victorian, very smartly entertaining. It was fun to have a beer there surrounded by reminders of one of our favorite literary characters. We both appreciated the importance of logic to Holmes.

The day of our appointment arrived. At the Natural History Museum, we were struck by the grandeur of the building, with its high ceilings and ornate architecture. No wonder it has been called "a cathedral of nature", being the world-renowned pre-eminent center for natural history and related research worldwide. In fact, the museum specialized in taxonomy, identification, and conservation. We learned that many of its collections had both historical and scientific value, including specimens collected by the renowned naturalist Charles Darwin.

We navigated to the section of the museum dedicated to small mammalian specimens, where we were greeted by the sight of countless drawered cabinets, each containing specimens of different small animal species.

After a few moments of searching, finally, Michael's keen eye spotted the hamster specimen he sought, Item BM(NH) 1855.12.24. 120. It was lying in a drawer with other hamster specimens, carefully labeled, and with its fur still somewhat intact and its tiny paws curled up as if in slumber. My husband carefully examined the animal, an elderly adult female from Aleppo, Syria.

As he studied it, he looked up at me and said in awe, "I can't believe I am actually touching the first hamster, the real 'type specimen' that defines the species of *Mesocricetus auratus Waterhouse*."

Michael Murphy studies the hamster "type specimen"

He recalled reading that George Robert Waterhouse, the Curator of London Zoological Society, presented this very specimen as a new species at a meeting of the Society on April 9, 1839. The new species was originally named *Cricetus auratus Waterhouse*, but the genus name was later modified to *Mesocricetus* due to taxonomic revisions for classifying hamsters as the understanding of the hamster species evolved.

Michael wondered how Waterhouse obtained it, and later in his career he investigated the question but never found it documented anywhere. He surmised that it might have come from Albert Russell, an early benefactor of the British Museum. Between 1740 and 1750 Russell was a practicing physician in Aleppo, Syria. In 1756 he published *The Natural History of Aleppo*, which contains a paragraph about a hamster he had dissected having cheek pouches full of French beans.

In his later research on the history of the hamster my husband learned that Waterhouse at age 21 was invited by Charles Darwin to join him on the voyage of the H. M. S. Beagle, but Waterhouse declined. However, upon his return Darwin convinced Waterhouse to catalog and describe the mammals and beetles that were collected on that expedition.

After spending some time studying the hamster specimen and taking some photographs of it, Michael reluctantly tore himself away. Inspired by exploring this animal's enigmatic past we were eager to travel to Syria and see where these animals live in the wild.

CHAPTER 4

Scouting in Lebanon

On May 12 we flew from London to Beirut, Lebanon, via Frankfurt and Istanbul. We took a taxi into the city, by chance sharing with a Japanese man. The taxi driver was very friendly and talked us into staying at a certain Cadmos hotel – "Pan Am special rate, half price" and we agreed to his choice because it was also located near the university. We planned to visit professors at the American University of Beirut. Michael had corresponded with several of them regarding his quest to find wild hamsters.

The first day or so we suffered culture shock, especially at dinnertime the first evening when we looked for a restaurant and randomly entered the front outdoor garden of one associated with the Excelsior Hotel. Not surprisingly, the waiters did not speak English. We were not offered a menu, but a waiter politely seated us in the lighted garden on a cushioned sofa fronted by a round copper coffee table. Here the waiter served us a small *mezza* (selection of Arab dishes) and *shish kebab*, which is a grilled skewer of meat and vegetables. We had never heard of *mezza*, but Michael was always eager to try new foods and enjoyed it all, while I gingerly tasted each dish and ate selectively. At the time, we were not told what we were being served or the price of the meal, but it was tasty and inexpensive, including wine.

As we explored Beirut, we learned that there were many excellent restaurants offering the international food we were accustomed to, such as Italian, French, or Chinese. In those restaurants, waiters often spoke English and we could select our meal from a menu, and some of the restaurants had live music, perhaps a strolling violinist or an instrumental trio.

In the coming days we experienced Beirut, the capital city of Lebanon, as an interesting and bustling metropolis. It was coming to life in the springtime, and the city was awash with the colors and fragrances of blooming flowers and trees. I was especially fond of the lavender-blue blooming jacaranda trees, their profusion of flowers filling their umbrella-like canopies. Perhaps because of my blue eyes, blue has always been my favorite color. The weather was mild and pleasant, with temperatures in the mid-60s to the low 80s Fahrenheit. The city's streets displayed a rich tapestry of culture and history, with diverse architecture ranging from ancient ruins to modern high-rises like our hotel. From such a high-rise building, one can admire the beautiful view of the Corniche, a curved seaside promenade in the Central District of Beirut. Encircling the Beirut promontory the route is lined with palm trees and provides awe-inspiring views of the brilliant blue Mediterranean.

On our second day there we conferred with the scientists at the American University of Beirut with whom Michael had corresponded. Originally established as the Syrian Protestant college in 1866, the American University of Beirut is a private, non-sectarian, and independent university chartered in New York. It opened on December 3, 1866, with its first class of 16 students. It was renamed the American University of Beirut in 1920. The university offered programs leading to bachelor's, master's, MD, and Ph.D. degrees, instruction being done in English. Currently, the campus has 64 buildings, including the American University of Beirut Medical Center. Its graduates reside in 120 countries throughout the world.

The university is perched on a hill overlooking the Mediterranean Sea on one side and bordering Bliss Street on the other to the south. The campus is an architectural mosaic, blending historic structures with modern facilities. It is located in the Hamra neighborhood, and Bliss Street is a lively thoroughfare. Here you will find numerous restaurants, cafes, and eateries, presenting a variety of foods from traditional Lebanese dishes to international cuisine. It is also a hub for students, locals, and visitors alike.

The broader neighborhood is known as Ras Beirut, a melting pot of history, diversity, and creativity. We enjoyed its cosmopolitan atmosphere, blending old world charm with modern sensibilities. We learned that Bliss Street, named after Dr. David Bliss, the university's first president, was a meeting point for students, professors, and intellectuals.

We tried to meet anyone who might have information about Aleppo or hamsters there. First we met Dr. Phillip Basson, George Kassis, and Bill Hayes in the Biology Department. We had lunch at nearby Uncle Sam's. Dinner that night was at Romano's 222, which had very good Italian food.

The next day we had breakfast at Uncle Sam's and met two students who conversed with us about the AUB school and about pollution. Upon returning, at the school entrance were several internal security policemen wearing red berets. We had to go to the back gate to enter the campus. Dr. Basson showed us the biology lab and the aquarium. Afterward we encountered Bill Hayes and his wife, and we all arranged to meet about 4 pm when they would take us to the *souqs,* the mid-eastern bazaar. Meanwhile, we had lunch at the university's "Milk Bar" and were pleased to meet the two students we had met earlier at breakfast. They pointed out the Psychology building. There we met a student from Sweden named Francesca von Vietinghoff, who introduced us to Professor Chimienti from Yale and a friend of his from Aleppo. We also contacted Dr. R. Mroueh at the School of Medicine and met George's brother, Amin Kassis. The Kassis brothers were from Aleppo and their father was a gynecologist there. We met several other teachers and students.

When we visited the Psychology Department the next day we visited with Dr. Chimiente and met Dale and Karen Atrens. We had lunch together and the Atrens' drove us south of the city to look for pottery and to shop briefly at a 'supermarket'. Later our new friend, Bill Hayes, with his wife Sandra took us in a service-taxi to see the *souqs*, and kindly entertained us for dinner at their home in a village outside of Beirut. It was a large new apartment, but required a long drive on a bad road. They showed us where a woman was making 'mountain bread,' a flat bread baked on a hot surface that appeared to be a rock. This rural woman was wearing traditional attire, a long dress with long sleeves, and no head scarf. It was evening and the glow from the cooking fire lent a picturesque quality to the scene.

Our new friends, Dale and Karen Atrens, showed us their nice 14th floor apartment in Beirut and invited us to attend a horse show at the Turf Club the next day. Perhaps we would meet someone who knew about Aleppo or the hamsters there. While at the Turf Club, Francesca, our new friend from the University, took us to the Arabian Horse Club to see the horses before the show. It might have been possible that people there knew of hamsters, because horse ranches are located in rural locations. We enjoyed the horse show and especially the ability to meet local people. Everyone was very friendly and helpful.

Francesca also introduced us to a couple of Arab men who might have heard of hamsters, but, unfortunately, they had not. One was Mr. Kamal Farajallah and the other a Bedouin named Hamid. Hamid was dressed in a suit, carried worry beads, and had a mustache. He never smiled. He had never seen hamsters, but took a photo to show the Bedouins so he could ask if they had seen hamsters. Mr. Farajalllah's wife,

Leonie, drove us to a pet store in Beirut where she had seen hamsters, and sure enough, they had several.

We also were approached by a young Palestinian boy, a refugee. He was selling small packets of Chiclets gum to earn a little money for his family. Michael was happy to oblige, and bought several packets.

At the university we chatted with some students at a picnic table in an outdoor courtyard under the dappled shade of trees. One fellow remarked that I was 'blond' according to the locals. My fair skin and light brown hair with red highlights were unusual there, and my blue eyes too. While my husband's soft dark brown hair and brown eyes were more the local norm.

Michael made friends easily, creating comradery with his great sense of humor. His friendly smile and quick wit turned strangers into friends in a flash. He dressed casually in a collared, button-down shirt or else rather neatly in white shirt and tie, slacks, and leather shoes, which would be normal for

Conferring with AUB students

a professor or professional person at the time. I always wore a dress with flats or sandals in Beirut, usually a sleeveless dress because of the warm weather. I pulled my long hair away from my face and secured that part of it in a barrette at the back leaving the rest of it to fall naturally.

We needed a rental car to make our way from Beirut to Aleppo, the second largest city in Syria, the locale where the original wild hamsters were caught. The crucial arrangement was made for a trusty Volkswagen Beetle, an unassuming yet dependable steed for our extraordinary journey. Our car at home was a VW. The gray-haired rental agent stated that the vehicle was on loan to us (for the usual fee) because rental cars were not allowed into Syria from outside. He explained that Syria had that rule to protect its own rental car businesses, although no such businesses existed at the time. The man gave us a personal letter describing that the car was being loaned to me, a college friend of the agent's daughter. The agent also checked our international driver's licenses and scribbled through the word "Israel," which was listed as one of the countries that accepted the license. This somewhat amused us, but we understood the acknowledgement of the region's political nuances.

The kindly rental agent came with us to the border and helped us get across. Our suitcases were searched at the border. My husband wondered if there would be trouble because of his insulin syringes, but the English word "sugar" was close enough to the Arabic *"sucar"* for the border agents to understand his diabetes.

They were more interested in the two-dozen folding aluminum live-capture animal traps, the likes of which they had never seen. Folded flat, a trap measured about 3 inches by 8 inches and about one-half inch thick. Michael showed them how the trap could be popped open to form a rectangular box. He set the front door of the trap and demonstrated with walking fingers how an animal might be caught inside it. It was so clever they wanted it demonstrated several times, and all had a great laugh. Thus, we were allowed to enter Syria.

One closed trap and one open trap

The rental agent was required to come with us beyond the border. He asked us to let him off at nearby Tell Khamin and said he would make his way home from there. He gave us the name of a border agent who could assist us when we returned. I jotted the name in the small date book I had brought for taking notes.

Now we were on our own in Syria. To us this was not much different from the time we were driving a rental car on the island of Crete last year. We had gotten a bit lost but eventually found our way back to Heraklion, the capital. We did not mind little adventures like that.

Now we wanted to learn as much as possible about Syria and its history. Soon we stopped briefly to visit Krak des Chevaliers, also known in Arabic as *Qalaat al Husn*, a picturesque 11th century crusader castle. A grizzled but friendly guide led us through labyrinthine corridors of the castle. With each step we imagined we retraced the footsteps of ancient warriors, imaging the clink of their swords against their armor. The guide pointed to the grand hall, once the heart of the fortress. Here knights had gathered to feast and strategize, their voices loudly echoing through the vaulted ceilings. We explored the kitchens, where hearty meals had fueled the defenders, and the stables where the warhorses had been groomed for battle. The guide adeptly brought the ruins to life with every word. We were able to take a fabulous photo of the entire castle crowning its hilltop on a glorious day.

Krak des Chevaliers, Syria

CHAPTER 5

Palmyra

Our route took us through the rustic city of Homs and across the desert to Palmyra. While out of the direct route to Aleppo, Palmyra was a necessary stop on the way in order to visit an archaeologist, Dr. Oleg Graber, with whom Michael had corresponded regarding working in Syria and had promised to visit him. We hoped he had information about hamsters in the country, or at least, perhaps he could provide some contacts in Aleppo who might be of assistance to us there.

We drove through Homs and decided not to stay but to continue to Palmyra. We noticed a kangaroo rat and a hedgehog on the road that evening. Arriving after sunset we were greeted by a breathtaking sight. The ancient ruins of tall columns, bathed in the glow of our headlights, stood as eerie yet magnificent sentinels guarding the once vibrant center of trade.

We were warmly welcomed at the Hotel Zenobia and had dinner with a waiter in constant attendance as though we were royalty. He would stand at attention behind my shoulder, his livery being a rather rumpled white cotton jacket, while we savored the flavors of traditional Syrian cuisine.

Hoping to learn more about Syria's history we enlisted a local guide in the morning to lead us through the ancient Greek and Roman ruins. He took us to the Temple of Bel, a Roman masterpiece dating from about 32 CE, where we sipped tea with the temple's keeper.

Palmyra

Here they outfitted us with the Syrian headdress that protects one from the searing desert sun in June. Atop Michael's typical black and white patterned headscarf, a meter square, called a *keffiyah*, was the standard black rope-like circlet called an *agal* or *igal* which keeps the scarf in place.

Janet's new headwear

Michaael's keffiyah

My circlet was four rounds deep, each round wound with colored cord in a pattern involving black, white, and gold bands. Red cord was woven to form a flexible separation between the inflexible pieces. This decorative circlet sat atop my white headscarf. It was so beautiful that I imagined this was what Queen Zenobia wore in about 270 CE when she attempted to free Palmyra from Roman rule during the reign of Claudius II.

At the museum we located the man with the keys to the tombs and then visited the Valley of the Tombs. We climbed up into a tower tomb, and we clambered around the underground tombs. One had a large modern pipe running through it. The hotel keeper's brother was Khaled al Asaa'd, the Museum Director, who served us tea and coffee at his house and offered to accompany us across the desert to Dr. Graber's archeological dig.

Under Dr. Asaa'd's knowledgeable direction we struck out and followed barely discernible tracks across the desert and through dry washes called *wadi*s. Once we were stopped by armed soldiers, which caused Michael and me some uneasiness, but the museum director greeted them and described our intent to visit the archaeologists working about 60 miles east of Palmyra.

Murphy and Asaa'd meet others in the desert

We later met a TV camera team from Damascus, who were doing a documentary on Dr. Graber's archeological site, the medieval Islamic town of Qasr al-Hayr al-Sharqi. Such was the traffic we encountered in that barren wasteland on a track we Americans could not detect, and each encounter merited stopping to meet and greet.

CHAPTER 6

Archaeological Site

The site emerged from the sands like a mirage. Earthen walls, weathered by time, enclosed enigmatic structures shaped like beehives. A solitary tent, its white fabric billowing in the gentle breeze, stood sentinel at the entrance. There Dr. Graber and the other archeologists welcomed us most cordially, saying they were glad to have visitors and new conversations. They showed us around the ancient caravanserai and town. Their bathroom was "over there, behind that shoulder-high wall." Talk about an outhouse! No roof, no door. "And be sure to sprinkle the lime appropriately," we were advised. In the evening we had a convivial dinner with them.

We slept on cots in the small white tent and were awakened quite early by one of their Muslim helpers, a black-robed Bedouin named Gaili, who had formed a square of large stones on the ground which I assumed to symbolize a mosque facing east, and he was kneeling in his "mosque"

Archaeological site of Qasr al-Hayr al-Sharqi

loudly chanting his morning prayers. Perhaps the square of stones did not represent a mosque, but rather, the Muslim prayer rug. In any case, I was quite happy to get up and out of the tent, even at such an early hour, when I noticed the large menacing scorpion under my cot!

We had a breakfast of pancakes with Dr. Graber. This interesting archaeologist was born in France in 1939 and spent most of his career in the United States, earning his Ph.D. from Princeton in 1955 and having an academic career including a full professorship at Harvard in 1980. Dr. Graber's archaeological and scholarly research covered a wide range of Islamic studies across Africa, the Middle East, and Muslim Asia, and he produced many scholarly publications. It was a pleasure to have a chance to visit with him and learn first hand how real archaeologists work.

We asked if he knew anything about hamsters in the area. We hoped he might have encountered them, but unfortunately, he had not. After breakfast Dr. Graber and an assistant showed us the few artifacts that they had found at this site. It looked like a collection of pottery fragments and perhaps some pieces of rudimentary tools. I felt sorry that they had so little to show for their hard work. However, to Dr. Graber ceramic fragments and rudimentary tools revealed glimpses of a sophisticated culture that had vanished centuries ago.

The museum director, Dr. Asaa'd, said he was staying with the archeologists for a few days, so he arranged for Abdullah, the adult son of a local sheik, to be our guide as we completed our drive across the desert. Abdullah was a tall, handsome Arab with a black mustache. He wore a long floor-length brown men's garment called a *thawb* with a gray suit coat over it. He had the black *agal* atop his solid white headscarf, which he wore with one end wrapped under his chin and tucked into the *agal* up on the other side. He sat in the front passenger's seat while Michael drove, and I occupied the back seat. Abdullah almost never said anything but would point the direction we were to go or say something that sounded like "*saywee*" to indicate we should proceed straight ahead.

We stopped for lunch at Resafa, which is famous for having large underground cisterns. The remains of timeworn arches cast intricate shadows on the sun-scorched earth. Some Arab tourists were there and were interested to hear what my guidebook said about the site.

It recounted that Resafa dates from the 9th century BCE, and during the Roman times it was once an opulent caravanserai on the trade routes linking Aleppo, Palmyra, and Dura Europos. Ruins of long arcades and a few scattered columns, once a mosque, stood above remnants of the an-

Resafa's famous cisterns

cient water system. Beneath the desert sands lay vast cisterns, their arched roofs still intact. Earlier they had quenched the thirst of weary travelers, now they stood empty, tempting the curious visitor to take a peek.

It was a mystery to us how Abdullah found his way across the empty wasteland, but he guided us directly to the dusty town of Raqqa. My guidebook noted that this historic town was the capital of the Abbasid Caliphate between 796 and 809 CE under the reign of Harun al-Rashid. It looked unimpressive to us now. But at least it was a town, a sign of people and civilization. We were glad to be out of the scalding expanse of desert.

Here Abdullah took his leave and went to find the American Mission people who would take him back home. We did all this without knowing a word of Arabic, or Abdullah a word of English!

Road to Aleppo

From Raqqa we found the road west to Aleppo, thankfully paved. It was just an old blacktop ribbon, lacking any painted markings. Occasionally I spotted a distance marker, which was a rectangular piece of concrete set upright on the ground beside the road, although many had fallen over. They were painted white in two sections, the left side reading Alep 130 (or the number of kilometers to go) and the right side reading the same in Arabic script. The road stretched out through the barren landscape, perhaps with a few weeds on the verge. Occasionally a donkey or two could be seen grazing there.

CHAPTER 7

Aleppo

Our base in Aleppo was the Hotel Baron, pronounced with the accent on the last syllable in the French manner. It was situated in the heart of Aleppo and was erected in 1911 by a pair of Armenian brothers named Mazloumian. Upon its inception, it was the first hotel in the region designed to cater to Western travelers. The iconic hotel boasted an imposing stone entrance terrace enclosed by a stone balustrade and featured a couple of intimate bistro sets, providing a pleasing ambiance.

Despite the passage of time, the Hotel Baron exuded a vintage grandeur, albeit with visible signs of wear on its carpets and furniture. Its rich history has drawn numerous notable figures over the years, including Agatha Christie, Lawrence of Arabia, King Faisal, Kemal Ataturk, and almost every Syrian president.

Although past its prime it was the best hotel in Aleppo. Koko Mazloumian, the owner, and the hotel's staff were very pleasant and accommodating. We stayed there almost four weeks and saw a lot of coming and going.

We ate nearly all our meals in the hotel's stately dining room, where our white-haired waiter moved with the precision of a clock. He exuded an air of quiet dignity as he served guests with unwavering formality. Michael delighted in teasing him by sometimes rotating his dinner plate such that the hotel insignia was no longer at the top where the waiter placed it. The waiter would always adjust the plate when he noticed it was askew. We believed that he understood the joke and played along. He had the upper hand when we ordered our meals from the French menu, Syria's second language being French. Almost no one there spoke English, and the closest we had to a second language was a little Spanish or German. Neither of us had studied French. Sometimes our meals were a surprise.

For a few days during our stay, the governors of the provinces of Turkey were meeting in Aleppo and were staying at the Hotel Baron. They liked to spend some free time playing backgammon in the hotel's small lounge. They called the game *shish-bish* (six-five) or *tauli* (tables). We enjoyed playing the game with them, and they liked instructing us on the best moves to make. Often, they would move for us if we were not quick enough.

This was a game my father had taught me. He had played it while stationed in the Solomon Islands during World War II as a Navy pilot. At that time, my dad's game board was a man's white handkerchief painted with the game board's pennant-shaped spaces. The set of small black buttons and white shirt buttons, together with a small pair of dice, would be wrapped in the handkerchief for a game he could carry in his pocket.

CHAPTER 8

Dr. Iskander Kassis

From the first day we were in Aleppo, May 22, we began to establish contacts to assist in our enterprise. We always politely referred to these people with their honorific, for example, Mr. or Dr. We were young and essentially students, while many who helped us were older or engaged in professions.

First, we contacted Dr. Iskander Kassis, a gynecologist who ran a clinic there and we visited him at his house. He also used the English version of his name, Alexander. He was the father of George and Amin Kassis, whom we had met at the American University in Beirut. Dr. Kassis was balding with gray hair, with an imposing demeanor tempered by a warm and welcoming nature.

German friend Ingeborg, Dr. Kassis, and Janet Murphy

He said, "I have heard of people getting rich finding grain in hamster holes in the ground." I thought this was unlikely but said nothing.

Perhaps we had different ideas of what it meant to be rich. Perhaps I was unaware of how large a hamster burrow could be.

Born in Aleppo in 1941, Dr. Kassis received his medical degree from the University of Damascus in 1966. In addition to his medical work, Dr. Kassis was also deeply involved in the world of Arabian horses. He owned a beautiful farm just outside Aleppo, where he bred and raised these majestic animals. He took us to see his stables, and he invited us to lunch the following day. His kindness and willingness to assist us were a testament to his generosity and unwavering support for our scientific quest.

CHAPTER 9

Dr. Gieo Orita

There was a Japanese camera crew taking photos of Dr. Kassis and his horses. Dr. Kassis introduced us to Dr. Gieo Orita, a Japanese veterinarian, who came to play a pivotal role in our expedition. He noted that his clinic could give us the correct papers for exporting any hamsters we captured. His contributions to our expedition extended beyond his veterinary expertise. He introduced us to prominent individuals in Aleppo, such as Mr. Fayek Bahhady of the Syrian Agriculture Ministry, who provided invaluable assistance.

We visited Dr. Orita at the veterinary clinic located at the edge of town. It was busy and noisy. There were sheep, goats, chickens, and other animals milling around with some local men, farmers, and veterinarians. Dr. Orita, a slight man of 38 wearing his white lab coat, greeted us with pleasure although he was very busy at the time.

We wondered how a Japanese veterinarian had found himself working in Aleppo. Dr. Orita was born in Japan in 1933 and received his veterinary degree from Hokkaido University in 1956. He began his career working for the Japanese government in various roles related to animal health and

Dr Orita, in white, at his clinic

welfare. He eventually joined the United Nations Food and Agriculture Organization (FAO) and was sent to Syria in 1965 to work on a project aimed at eradicating the cattle disease rinderpest.

While in Aleppo, Dr. Orita quickly became known for his expertise. He worked tirelessly to educate local farmers and veterinarians about best practices in animal husbandry, and his efforts led to significant improvements in animal health and productivity. Dr. Orita also played a key role in establishing the Aleppo branch of the Syrian Veterinary Association, which helped to promote veterinary education and research in the region.

In addition to his work with animals, Dr. Orita was also deeply interested in the culture and history of Syria. He studied Arabic and developed a deep appreciation for the country's rich heritage and traditions. After leaving Syria, Dr. Orita continued to work for the FAO in various countries around the world. He eventually retired in 1998 and returned to Japan, where he remained active in the veterinary community.

While we were at his clinic Dr. Orita enlisted the help of the farmers to aid in our search for hamsters. They called the animal "father of the saddlebag" in reference to the hamster's immense cheek pouches. The hamster fills its cheeks with grain or other food or nesting materials and carries it to its burrow to store for later use. It has been reported that they can carry at least their body weight in those pouches. Later we learned that the formal Syrian name for the golden hamster is "ḥamstir ḏahabī", which directly translates to "golden hamster."

The hamster's namesake saddlebag

The saddlebag referred to by the Syrian farmers was a huge cloth or canvas carrier thrown across the back of a donkey. Both sides would be stuffed like a pillow to over-brimming with field products. We saw a young woman seated atop such a load as though riding a horse, clutching the bridle reins in one hand and a farm implement in the other. Her stockings and well-worn slippers showed beneath her skirt and her colorful headscarf was loosely wrapped, a good protection from the hot sun.

CHAPTER 10

Mr. Fayek Bahhady

Dr. Orita took us and Dr. Kassis to see Mr. Fayek Bahhady of the Planning Office for the Syrian Agriculture Ministry. He became an extremely essential part of our trip. He facilitated our visits to farms and served as interpreter during our contacts with farmers.

Fayek Bahhady

Dr. Orita and Mr. Bahhady took us 18 kilometers out of town to the Ministry of Agriculture farm, where we met a worker who said they caught hamsters in the fields near his village. He told us the animals ate the watermelon roots and stalks. The farmland was flat and seemed to stretch forever into the distance with its thick blanket of golden grain. We decided to come back later at 5 pm to see the village and fields at a time when the hamster was known to be active.

Hamsters stay in their burrows during the heat of the day. They come out to forage when the sun has gone down in the evening or early in the morning. Night activity is their only drawback as a pet. While they do not make noisy sounds themselves, one will often hear the squeaking of their exercise wheels in their cages at night.

We returned to Dr. Kassis' house and walked to the Strand Restaurant for lunch with him. He seemed to know everyone there, and he had a friendly conversation in Arabic with the owner of the restaurant. This was our first introduction to a restaurant we would visit very often during our stay in Aleppo.

CHAPTER 11

Visiting Fields and Farmsteads

Our journey involved extensive collaboration with local farmers and visits to numerous farmsteads or villages. These interactions provided invaluable insights into the local culture and hamster habitats. At the hotel we prepared the metal traps, and when Mr. Bahhady arrived at 4:30 pm on this day we drove to the farm director's house, had tea, and went to the village fields.

Having tea was almost always necessary when we visited someone's home. It allowed everyone to be friendly and take stock of each other, but it delayed the accomplishment of any task. This interlude was pleasant, and at the same time annoying, to the direct, efficient, and goal-oriented American way. My husband and I learned to slow down and be polite.

We searched for hamster burrows but did not find any. After visiting the village, we returned and set our traps in the government fields. We all ate strawberries fresh from the field, a real treat!

Mr. Bahhady offered to take us to his church the next day, Sunday, where they pray in Aramaic. We were extremely sorry to have missed that, but unfortunately, we were both sick the whole next day, probably from the unwashed strawberries. Dr. Kassis visited us in the hotel that afternoon at 2:30,

Murphy, Bahhady, and two farmers

3:30, and 10:10, and wrote a prescription in Arabic to treat our amoebic dysentery.

The ensuing day we went with Mr. Bahhady to check the traps. We caught three field mice, but no hamsters, and we lost one trap. At Mr. Bahhady's suggestion we made an appointment to see Anton Tahan, a teacher at Aleppo College, later that afternoon.

At Aleppo College we met Mr. Butros Makkoul, the Director, who told us where they caught the animal known as Shepherd's hamster. He said the animals come out early in the morning, and that it was very dry and rocky at that place, but that it was near a field. Machines were used on the field, which might have kept the hamsters from making their burrows in the field itself. He suggested, "you can leave your traps set at night and return in the morning to check them".

We returned to the hotel for lunch and a short nap. Dr. Kassis came by to check briefly on our health. We were extremely grateful for his care.

That afternoon we picked up Mr. Bahhady and went to our appointment with Mr. Tahan. Although he said he did not know of the hamster, we noticed that he had one in a jar of formaldehyde on the shelf in his lab. My husband gave a short scientific talk to the students, which Mr. Bahhady translated. Mr. Bahhady directed us as we drove to the village of Benyameen, where Mr. Butros Makkoul had said he had heard there might be hamsters. The villagers in Benyameen were familiar with hamsters, but said they were hard to find, although one man said he killed ten last year. Was this boasting to the foreigners?

We were fond of this village as it had friendly people and a pretty minaret. The children of the village gathered around and were very excited at having foreigners in their midst. At last, we drove rather far from a village, and put traps in an unused field where we found some holes that the Kurdish farmer, Ali, identified as belonging to hamsters. The next day we returned to check the traps, but they were all empty. We collected the traps and drove to another village where Ali showed us a field having hamster holes. He even tried to dig up one of the holes. After some discussion and consideration, the men finally decided to put the traps out in a different field.

CHAPTER 12

Ali's Farmstead

Ali's farmstead had several buildings of mudbrick. Main buildings were rectangular with flat roofs. There were also a few beehive shaped structures. If we had spoken their language we could have asked about the farmstead. Was it a village, a farmstead, a single family's farm? They called the settlement Blaht.

We noted that the women herded and milked sheep. I remembered the delicious cheese atop our salads in the hotel dining room. It must have been sheep cheese, and it tasted like a mild version of feta cheese. Michael and I both loved it and when ordering salad at restaurants we usually asked for the sheep cheese on the side to be added to the salad.

Woman tending the sheep

Ali with his children

Ali invited us into his house, and we sat on blankets on the floor with the *Hadji*, their grandfather, we assumed. Perhaps he was their father, but he looked old, venerable. We learned that *Hadji* was a title used for a man who had made the pilgrimage to Mecca, called the *hadj*. They served us tea and *leban* (yogurt) and mountain bread, the flat bread baked on an open stone, like that we had encountered in Beirut. The tea is usually served in small glasses, to which you add heaping spoonfuls of sugar. We always asked for our tea without the sugar, which amazed our hosts. But we both really preferred it that way, and sugar was bad for Michael's diabetes. Otherwise, we might have gone along with the local custom. I hoped they were not offended when we politely refused the sugar. Perhaps the fact that we were foreigners allowed us to perpetrate small departures from customs like that.

Outside, Michael took photos of Ali and his family with our Polaroid camera and gave them the instant photos as gifts. Ali motioned that he would like to buy the camera. We understood, but we thought that he would not be able to get the film for it in Aleppo. Therefore, we tried to indicate that this problem was the reason we could not honestly let him buy it from us. This was all said with our hands and shrugging of shoulders due to our lack of a language in common. Despite our ignorance of each other's spoken language, we became friends with Ali and his family.

Woman at Blaht

CHAPTER 13

Daily Work and Social Activities

We settled into a routine of visiting village, farmsteads, or local people to inquire about hamsters. Even when no hamsters were obtained we had interesting interactions with the people we met. Interspersed with those activities we endeavored to take some time to relax with our new friends or to explore the vicinity, especially ancient historic sites.

We were pleased to have been invited to attend a soiree at the French Consulate one evening. We walked there from our hotel and were ushered from the entry into a large room where about twenty people were gathering for hors d'oeuvres. Everyone was speaking French, of course, so we could only smile pleasantly for most of the time. The entertainment followed, a film in French about raising racing horses, and a film of The Marriage of Figaro opera. We enjoyed the films despite them being in French. Dr. Kassis was there and drove us back to the hotel afterwards.

The next day we checked the traps and found that we had caught a live hedgehog, which we took to Mr. Tahan at Aleppo College, who, we sadly found, immediately put it in a jar of formaldehyde to drown. I was envisioning that he would put it in a cage to observe its behavior or at least introduce the species to his students. I wished we had let it go free upon finding it in our trap. It was an endearing animal and I feared that its death this way would serve no purpose. I swallowed hard and kept quiet.

In the afternoon we took along a young hotel employee, Ahmed, when we visited Ali's village to set traps in a different location full of burrows. A big rainstorm and heavy wind prevented this endeavor. Ali took us to another village, called Kubara, where we were guests in a house and had tea with our hosts. There were foil pictures of Nasser and pretty rugs hung on the walls. We sat on the carpeted floor in a circle and discussed hamsters. I say this figuratively, as we spoke nothing but English and they spoke Kurdish or Arabic, so ignorant were we that we did not know which. We set some traps and drove home in the dark.

When Mr. Bahhady was not able to join us the next morning Michael and I drove alone to meet Ali and check the traps. We had caught a large, long-tailed lizard and a frog, which we let go. We also caught a glimpse of a hedgehog in his hole. We took more Polaroid photos of the family. Ali tried to flush some animals from their burrows using water, but we saw only field mice.

Ali's brother played his drum for us

The family kindly invited us again for tea in their house. Ali's adult brother played his large tambourine-like drum for us. We took more Polaroids for them, something the whole family always enjoyed. One time they grouped together for a large family group photo. Usually, Michael wielded the Polaroid and I snapped with the Nikon. After this nice visit we went back to the hotel for lunch.

Always the farmers showed us where they often saw the animals and we laid our traps, baited with a dab of peanut butter. Sadly, we never caught hamsters in those traps. But Ali was able to capture a hamster for us by throwing the fabric of his garment over the animal as it tried to run away. He indicated that this was easier when the animal was trying to cross an irrigation ditch. He put it in an empty 5-gallon tin can and presented it to us when we returned to check the traps the next day, Saturday, May 29.

Michael holds the first hamster caught

For my part, I captured Michael's delight in a photograph of him with his first wild Syrian golden hamster. He holds it by the loose skin behind the neck, the correct way to hold a hamster. This is also the way the hamster mother holds her babies. I snapped another of Michael with the farmer, Ali, who caught it.

We took the hamster to show Mr. Bahhady because we were so pleased. He went to the fields with us that afternoon, and in the evening we all had a celebration dinner at a restaurant he recommended, where we sat in the garden and had wine and a *mezza*. He introduced us to his co-worker, Antoine Istanbuli, and we all went to what he called a 'stereo club' after dinner. There we listened to recorded music as we visited and sipped our libations.

Ali met us at his village the next day and presented us with a hamster captured at Kubara. Michael

Ali and Michael Murphy with the hamster Ali caught

paid Ali for the hamster, 10 Syrian lira (about $2.50), plus 25 Syrian lira to Ali for his assistance.

Once Arman Mazloumian, the hotel owner's son, came with us to the Ansari area and to Ali's village, Blaht, to check the traps. Later we dropped off Arman at the hotel and went with Dr. Orita and his assistant to another part of the Ansari area to ask some farmers to look for hamsters. We also stopped at the police station to ask them too.

One man said they saw white hamsters, and that some villagers ate the white ones. We were not sure what animal they meant, because hamsters are not white. In fact, they are known for their beautiful golden coats. Perhaps they were referring to the animal's white chest. That afternoon Mr. Bahhady took us to Benyameen, and we also stopped on the road toward Zerbeh to question the villagers regarding hamsters – to no avail.

We had dinner at the Strand and later picked up Mr. Bahhady and went to Dr. Orita's house for drinks, fruit, and desserts. He had a beautiful apartment with five rooms and two servants. We all sat in his living room and visited. He presented me with a large Japanese pearl as a gift. I was overwhelmed by such a gift, and he could tell I was pleased.

Dr. Orita's teenaged son amazed us with his language abilities; he could speak, read, and write in Japanese, Arabic, and English. We were especially amazed at his ability because those three languages are written in different scripts and in different directions on the page.

I had an Arabic/English dictionary and referred to it often. But when looking up a word I heard in Arabic I never found it there. The dictionary was more useful for translating something from English into Arabic. In most Western countries my four years of high school Spanish and one year of college German were very useful for getting around, although I never conquered a foreign language fluently. I enjoy learning foreign languages, with my mathematical mind considering them a sort of code. I always tried to pick up some Arabic terms while we were in Aleppo. And some words like *hadj*, *leban*, *mezza*, and *wadi*, became part of my vocabulary in daily use. But, in truth, Arabic with its strange script was outside my untutored ability. On my own I only managed to decode the written numbers from one to nine.

On our way back from the field the next day we stopped to take photos of the Aleppo city name signs on the road and the view of Aleppo from the outskirts. Aleppo was a large city with modern apartment buildings in some areas. Our hotel was in the old part of the city, where traffic bustled on small streets. Traffic there consisted of cars, motorcycles, bicycles, buses, and also donkeys and camels. Pedestrians were everywhere. Many of the women wore the black full-length *niqab* or *burqa* with their face completely covered except for a small slit for the eyes. I worried about their safety when crossing streets in that traffic while their vision was restricted by their garb.

The strict dress code for women is not dictated by the Koran. From my experience in Syria, I thought it was accepted by women because the men are often rude and crude regarding women. Perhaps it is easier to live covered from head to toe than always swatting away stray hands and suffering impolite comments, which I endured from time to time while there. Most of the women I interacted with were Kurdish, foreign, or educated, and they followed a more free style of dress. I never interacted with a fully covered woman, and I expect we would have found it very difficult to understand each other without the benefit of facial expressions.

Roman road

About 45 kilometers west of Aleppo is one of the longest stretches of Roman road still existing. It was part of the main highway from Antioch to Chaeis at its time. When we encountered it one day we tried to drive our Volkswagen on it but had to back up when the road ended at least a foot higher than ground level. But it tickled us that we had actually driven on a Roman road.

We stopped at Dr. Orita's clinic and watched the doctors remove an abnormal stillborn sheep from its mother. We showed the live hamster we had with us to the farmers there, and they promised to try to catch them for us. We also met the Chief of Police and showed him the hamster. After lunch at the Strand we went to the *souqs* and did some shopping.

CHAPTER 14

Shopping at the Souqs

For me, the best part of being in Aleppo were the *souqs*, the huge historic covered bazaar in the heart of Aleppo. Collectively called the Al-Medina Souq, it was the largest covered historic market in the world. It had several alleys and cross lanes totaling about 13 kilometers, mostly cobbled, and all lined with separate vendors' stalls. Historically, the larger *souq* would consist of *khans* (caravanserais) which were named after their specialty, for example, the wool *souq* or the leather *souq*. It was much the same now. Many of these are quite old, one dating to 1450.

A typical part of the Aleppo souq

In the *souqs* you could find whole sheepskins, large bundles of fresh garlic, oriental carpets, decorated fabrics, table linens, and garments, jewelry, beautiful wooden inlaid work, ceramics, and much more. We were obviously foreigners, and the shop keepers would try to get my attention by calling to me in French "madame, madame." We learned to haggle to obtain a lower price, and always felt better after paying less, even though we knew the shop keeper also felt he had pulled one over on us.

I learned to barely glance at the item I desired, idly asking the price, and then moving my attention to another item whose price I also asked. When I made an offer and the shop keeper's responding price was not satisfactory, I feigned loss of interest. Often Michael would play the husband's role, telling me we did not need the item or could not afford it, and often the shopkeeper would lower the price again. It seemed like a kind of dance.

Broom seller in the Aleppo souq

Many of the shop stalls were beautiful in their array of colorful offerings, be they fabrics, garments, or even spices. They often displayed wares in neat patterns, such as rows of straw brooms, or tidy pyramidal stacks of fresh fruits. We avoided the meat market stalls, however. There one could see flies buzzing around the carcasses hung from the rafters, and the smell was not pleasant.

Back to work we checked with the boy in the field the next day, and again showed villagers at Dr. Orita's clinic the live hamster. For something different Mrs. Kassis and a German friend named Ingeborg Zaremba took me to the *souq* where we looked at carpets. This shop had several stacks of carpets laid flat and many single carpets, rolled and set on end, lining the walls of the room. The shopkeeper would ceremoniously throw the carpet so it unrolled toward you with a flourish. One after another, until one really caught your interest. Ingeborg loved the oriental carpets and bought one to take back to Berlin with her.

I was young and my taste ran more to Scandinavian simplicity at the time, although now I greatly admire, even covet, lovely oriental carpets and have several in my home.

My husband and I had lunch at the Strand and were going to tour a little for a change. But a man at the Strand said there were hamsters in his village. We took teenaged Armen Mazloumian and young Hassan from the hotel as guides to find the village. With the boys directing we drove in that direction, and at one point found ourselves driving in a dry stream bed over large boulders. This was absolutely foolhardy! If we blew a tire, in all probability we would not be able to change it. It was at this point we decided that, as Michael wryly said, "this particular hamster location is not convenient enough for our needs." And we headed back to Aleppo and the hotel. We did not mind if the boys had "taken us for a ride" because it was an interesting adventure that had us all laughing, and we got back safely, although nearly out of gas.

It was Michael's birthday – June 3. We checked for hamsters at Abdul's and stopped at Dr. Orita's clinic. A man was there from Zerbeh who had brought us a wild hamster, for which he wanted 20 Syrian lira. We returned to the hotel and left the animal in its 5-gallon can abode in our room. After paying our two-week hotel bill we went to register with the police – what a madhouse! It was crowded and noisy. We dreaded returning on Saturday to pick up our passports.

CHAPTER 15

Aleppo Citadel and Cultural Encounters

To learn more about the history of Aleppo we stopped to visit the Aleppo Citadel, an imposing structure atop a hill near the center of the old town. It has a monumental gateway at the entrance, and one enters first through this gatehouse before passing through the principal entranceway.

Aleppo Citadel

In ancient times this was a fortified acropolis. Several times captured, most of the Citadel remains that we saw date from the Muslim conquest of 636 CE. The Citadel was difficult to conquer and those who managed to take it usually did massive reconstruction and improvements on the site.

We enjoyed our tour with a friendly guide who tried to teach us a little Arabic. We explored the baths and the courtyard. The guide said the king's throne room was being remodeled for a museum. We looked inside the dark cisterns and toured the dungeon, imagining the horrors of being incarcerated there. When we visited the small mosque our guide stressed that it was in this place that Abraham milked his gray cow. Why was that important? I looked it up later and learned that in Arabic the city of Aleppo is called *Halab*. Some say this comes from the word *halaba*, which means "gave out milk," there being an ancient tradition that Abraham of the Old Testament gave milk to travelers in this center of ancient commerce and trade.

Later we went to Blaht to see Ali. He had two hamsters for us, one alive and one dead. A friend of Ali's named Gamal Abdullah rode back with us to Aleppo and on the way took us to his house for fruit and tea. He was very proud of his wife. She had several shiny gold teeth, and he had paid a hefty bride price for her, 5000 Syrian lira (about $1136). They were amazed that I had come with my husband on this trip. How long had we been married? How many children did we have? Where were our children? When I indicated that we had been married for four years and had no children, they were aghast, and said I should see a doctor. So we said everything was really all right and that we wanted two children and that if we had them my mother would look after them while we were gone. We did not want to attempt a conversation about birth control. The whole discussion was done by hand waving and head nodding.

I felt that my actions were often not in adherence with the local role of the female. I wore casual pants outfits, which were currently in vogue back home in the U.S. In this way I considered myself discreetly covered. Once, when we were walking down the street two men behind us pelted me in the back with pistachio nuts, perhaps trying to get my attention or to see what would happen. They surely knew that they were being unkind to a foreign woman. It was quite childish.

"Michael, that man is throwing nuts at me!" I was angry about it, and felt it was extremely rude, but my wise husband advised me to pretend not to notice because we were very near our destination and would soon avoid the problem. I continue to wonder, however, what cultural norms and personal beliefs would lead an adult man to treat any stranger with such disrespect and unkindness.

Now I believe that my presence on the expedition might have been a problem at times, even risky. We had not considered that we would be working in places where females were rarely seen, such as the veterinary clinic or farmers' fields. And my being a foreign female made it even more rare. We often drew a lot of attention, which I attributed simply to our being foreigners, but might have been exacerbated by one of us being a woman.

Michael and I thought of ourselves as a close team, loving partners in all endeavors. We always aided and supported each other. Michael was invariably supportive of women in his profession, and in women's rights in general. It never occurred to us that a female should not accompany him on this expedition. In truth, I was a great help to him.

Another cultural difference seemed to be that the American use of time was too efficient for the people we met. They liked to haggle, or at least converse, over every decision. I fear that we were often acting rudely when we tried to complete a bit of business quickly, without the normal give and take. We learned to force ourselves to conduct our business more leisurely.

CHAPTER 16

Exploring Around Aleppo

I had decided to take Dr. Orita's gift pearl to be set as a ring. We visited the recommended jeweler and ordered a ring in white gold with a design that matched my wedding rings.

We also visited the rather new National Museum that morning, and thought it was very nicely done. Exhibits were neatly displayed in modern cases complete with informative labels. We appreciated the lay-out, because a single route through the museum could cover all the ex-hibits without any backtracking. It contained exhibits of remains from the myriad ancient civilizations of the Near East – Hittite, Sumerian, Mitannian, Hurrian, Assyrian, Phoenician, and others.

Remains of St. Simeon's pillar in the church at Qalaat Simeon

After lunch we drove to Qalaat Simeon, where a guide showed us around. This is an interesting ruin near Aleppo which includes the pillar atop which St. Simeon Stylites (386 – 459 CE) perched on a 6-foot square platform for 37 years or more as a Christian holy man and ascetic. A church was built around the column in 490 CE, and its ruins can be explored. Not much of the pillar remains, just a stone about 3 or 4 feet high set up on a plinth.

Here my husband was especially taken with the eggs and spears motif, representing female and male, also life and death, which is ubiquitous as decoration in ancient times. Being of Scotch-English ancestry I was drawn to the large carved stone Celtic cross. Some of the columns of the church were Corinthian style, but with wind-blown acanthus leaves, a style typical of north Syrian architecture.

Back in Aleppo, we received an invitation to visit the hotel owner's apartment for drinks and snacks after dinner that evening. There we met with Mr. Koko Mazloumian and his wife, two English girls from Beirut, and the German Vice-Consul and his wife. It was an interesting evening of friendly conversation. Nearly all of the conversation was in English, out of respect for those of us who did not speak any other language. We greatly enjoyed the visit and appreciated their kindness to us.

Wind-blown acanthus leaves

One day we went to Mr. Bahhady's office and found there was a hamster brought from Benyameen. Mr. Bahhady's colleague, Antoine Istanbule, accompanied us on our errands throughout the rest of that day as we visited the fields.

Janet inspects a new carrying case for six hamsters

Now that we had hamsters, we needed to arrange for transporting them to the United States. Hamsters need to be housed separately because they fight, especially if a male and female are housed together. Michael designed a carrier box divided into 6 compartments arranged 2 by 3 on a side, with a single screened lid hinged to cover the whole, and a leather handle on the side so it could be carried like a suitcase. He took the design to a carpenter and ordered two boxes to be constructed. The carpenter did a nice job and even used white-sided plywood making the outside of the boxes look very nice.

Mr. Istanbule took us to a kebab place for lunch. He met us again at 5 pm for a quick trip to Blaht, but they had no hamsters that day.

My husband had decided to pay the farmers for each live hamster they caught, since they produced better results than the metal traps. Each day we would visit several villages to see if any hamsters were caught. We obtained several 5-gallon tin cans with their tops removed where we kept the hamsters in our hotel room. We provided the animals with fresh food, water, and a small amount of bedding. Fortunately, hamsters are not noisy or smelly, but we wondered what the hotel maids thought about their animal guests.

We kept trying to contact people who could lead us to hamsters. Antoine Istanbule introduced us to a friend who owned a farm near Blaht, who would take us there the next day. Again, we visited Dr. Orita's clinic, where we met a man who said he would try to catch them for us. We also met a young fellow who was studying English literature at the University, who offered to take us north to Azzaz and Kurdish territory. We ate, picked up our passports at the police station, and drove out the road toward Azzaz. Along the way we saw the guide for Qalaat Simeon and gave him a ride. We stopped in Tel Rafat and crowds surged around us. But the people there had only seen Turkish hamsters, which are smaller and have dark coats rather than the golden color. They are a separate species and do not crossbreed with Syrian hamsters.

Back in Aleppo we had lunch at the Strand, visited the *souqs*, and played backgammon in the hotel lounge. Gamal Abdullah came by to tell us he could take us to another village tomorrow. When Mr. Bahhady phoned, we arranged to go to dinner together. We sat in the restaurant garden for a while, ate inside, and enjoyed the excellent food. There was a jazz band and the singing was in Armenian.

My husband was sick the next day and he could not go with Gamal Abdullah to his village. I took the Volkswagen that afternoon and drove to Mr. Bahhady's office to ask if he would go with me to Blaht. Both he and Mr. Istanbule decided to come along. I drove but at one point there was a large *wadi* to cross.

"I am not sure the VW can do it," I said. Mr. Bahhady volunteered to drive over it, and after we were safely across, he relinquished the driving back to me. At the time I knew that it might be unusual for women to drive. I give those two men credit for treating me with respect and politeness as they would have another male.

We visited two villages there, and also stopped at Blaht, where our friends said they followed a hamster to its hole and would try to catch it.

At Benyameen they had another hamster for us. I paid 20 S.L. for each. It was good that we made the trip, because I brought back two newly captured hamsters to Michael's delight. His face really lit up.

One day my husband and I were in the hotel lounge playing backgammon, when the hotel owner, Mr. Mazloumian, came to say that a friend of his was here and wanted to meet us because he was also a psychologist. Mr. Mazloumian left us to visit with the man for a while in the lounge. My husband was delighted to meet another person with an education in psychology, and the man expressed interest in our project.

We had a nice visit, but after he left Michael remarked to me, "for a psychologist that fellow has very little knowledge of the field."

Later he commented to the desk clerk regarding the visitor and was told that the man was really from an agency like the "Syrian CIA", checking to see what we were actually doing there. That made sense, but we did not worry, because we were obviously doing what we said we were.

When we next visited Dr. Orita's clinic we were besieged by men, but found that they were soldiers taking classes nearby, and had no knowledge of hamsters. Did we arouse such interest because they found a foreign woman in a place where only men might be expected to be?

CHAPTER 17

Jewelry Shopping

We had a leisurely day of shopping. We checked to see if my pearl ring was ready yet and went to the gold *souq* to buy Armenian silver jewelry. The price was based on the weight of each piece.

One very pretty necklace had a six-pointed star on the pendant, and I naively remarked, "that resembles the Jewish star." Immediately, the owner took the necklace from me, and with a pair of metal shears he cut the flat silver pendant in two with a flourish.

Janet shops for jewelry in the Aleppo souqs

The necklace I finally bought featured a flat triangular silver pendant decorated with small silver flowers at each corner and a tiny, decorated turquoise in the center of the triangle. Five flat simple silver flower-shaped pieces dangled from across the triangle's bottom. The chain of the necklace was quite heavy and ornate. The piece was unlike anything I had ever seen and appeared very Arabic and foreign to me. Whenever I wear it, I must polish the silver first.

The next day we reconnoitered near Azzaz and the Turkish border, were lost for a time, and finally found our way back. The day after that I was sick, and Michael did the morning chores. We picked up the pearl ring that afternoon and bought an enamel fish necklace pendant and a butterfly stick pin from the same jeweler. We drove to Blaht, where the people in the tent near the main road had an Armenian hamster, an animal that is not even in the same genus as the Syrian hamster. At Ali's they had a baby golden hamster, plus an adult. On the way back to Aleppo the people with the Armenian hamster stopped us because they had just caught a golden hamster for us.

CHAPTER 18

Visit to the Mediterranean Coast

It was Friday, June 11, and we had been away from home for over a month. We decided to take a day off. First we retrieved the traps from Abdul's field. As usual, no hamsters. Then we took a drive to Latakia on the coast taking Mr. Bahhady and Mrs. Cheryl Waggoner, a fellow hotel guest. It was a beautiful drive over mountains and through forests, and we stopped once for tea. We reached the town of Latakia and had lunch at a seaside restaurant – fish and *mezza*. We drove to Ugarit Beach and changed into swimwear in the bathhouse. We relaxed and enjoyed the warm water of the Mediterranean, the bright sun, and the sandy beach. It only cost 1 S.L. each, about 25 cents.

We changed back to street clothes and went to tour the Ugarit ruins, Ras Shamra, located about 6 miles (10 km) north of Latakia. It is situated on a large artificial mound. The site dates back to 6000 BCE, thus it is one of the earliest known urban centers. It reached its golden age and the height of its civilization between 1450 BCE and 1200 BCE. There we entered a tomb under a house, and we saw the room where the first alphabet was found in 1928. We learned that it was about 1400 BCE when the scribes in Ugarit began using 30 cuneiform-like letters representing sounds, now known as the Ugaritic alphabet. Each cuneiform symbol represented a single sound, 37 being consonants and three being vowels. It was written from left to right in syllables.

The earliest transcribed music was also found there. The music was inscribed on clay tablets using Ugarit cuneiform. One nearly complete tablet contains the Hurrian Hymn to Nikkal, the goddess of orchards, with lyrics and instructions for a singer accompanied by a nine-stringed sammüm, a type of lyre or harp.

We were fascinated by our visit to Ugarit, having an interest in learning the history of civilization. It was a great topic for conversation on the way back and when we stopped for a Syrian dinner in the town of Idlib.

In the morning Michael checked in at Dr. Orita's. After lunch we played some backgammon in the hotel lounge. Two men came by, saying they had caught two white hamsters at Hassaka. We all went to Mr. Istanbule's office for a translation of their story. He did not believe them, but we bought the hamsters and drove the men to their homes. When we visited Blaht Ali had two more wild Syrian golden hamsters for us. The next day while Michael was out the same two men with the white hamsters came by again at 10:40 am. I asked them to return at 1 pm with the two hamsters, and they said they could bring ten. While I stayed at the hotel and had lunch with Cheryl, Michael visited Mr. Bahhady and then Dr. Orita with the men. They all decided that the men were lying and that the hamsters were useless, as they were probably not wild.

Catholic Incarnation Procession in Aleppo

Later we went with Cheryl and Mr. Bahhady to see a Catholic Incarnation Procession. We met a man there who asked if we would like to see it from his balcony, so we had a wonderful view of the parade. Boys threw cracker-balls and confetti. We had dinner at the hotel with Cheryl and visited with Sirhan Mazloumian.

CHAPTER 19

Leaving Aleppo

In the morning of June 14, we went to Ali's farmstead to bid them farewell. They showed us their fruit trees and we took more Polaroid photos for them. On the way back, the village near the road had a hamster for us, for which we paid 15 S.L.

We went to Dr. Orita's, and he argued again with the men with the white hamsters, and he sent them away. He invited us for drinks in the evening. We got leather straps to put around the cage boxes at Mr. Bahhady's office. After lunch we bought several bottles of liquor as a gift for Mr. Bahhady, a nice gift since he was not Muslim. We picked him up at his office and took him to his apartment building and said our good-byes. We spent some time at the *souqs*, buying inlaid boxes, backgammon boards, and jewelry. At Dr. Orita's that evening we discussed colleges in America.

The next morning we said good-bye with heartfelt thanks to the people at the hotel, and we bade farewell to our friend Cheryl Waggoner, who had accompanied us to the Mediterranean coast. We also stopped at Dr. Orita's to take our final leave. By that time my husband had been provided with the official documents that he needed for exporting the hamsters.

With the hamsters safely ensconced in their fancy carrying boxes we took care that they did not get overly hot on the trip. For example, we left car windows open for a good breeze to come through the vehicle. As we drove out of Aleppo I was struck by the difference between the way of life in Aleppo and that in Boston. A huge difference! We drove on a rural blacktop road, encountering only a few farm buildings and farm animals. We passed a large wagon piled high with hay and pulled by mules. We drove past a few beehive shaped farm buildings until even they were left behind. I felt faintly nostalgic about leaving Aleppo and our friends there.

Janet rests with a view of nurias

Michael decided that we could stop in Hama for a short break. Hama is one of the oldest cities in the world, once the capital of an Aramean kingdom later conquered by Sargon in 720 BCE. We had stopped here to view the wonderful giant waterwheels, called *nurias*. *Nuria* is an Arabic word meaning "wheel of pots." These water wheels are powered by the river's current and have existed here since at least Byzantine times. They carry the water up from the Orantes River into aqueducts for irrigating the agricultural fields. The largest was an impressive 69 feet in diameter, and several were still in use after centuries. It was fascinating to see them still working.

We stopped later in Homs for lunch. At the Syrian border we asked for Mr. Fatallah, as previously instructed by the Beirut car rental agent, and he fixed up our car trip ticket with the usual *baksheesh* (tip). We got through the Lebanese border and drove as quickly as possible to Beirut hoping to ar-

Nuria in Hama

rive before the American University biology department closed. It was fortunate that Beirut time was an hour earlier than Syrian time, and Michael breathed a sigh of relief when we arrived at the university. In the Psychology department there Michael was able to put the animals in separate cages. The single animal that died was put in formaldehyde. After a few phone calls we checked into the upscale St. George Hotel, partly because their swimming pool was operative, which sounded very inviting after a long hot drive.

Michael settles his hamsters at the university temporarily

We visited the offices of TWA and Lufthansa the next day and arranged our airline tickets. Michael talked to the cargo man at Lufthansa, who said the hamsters could travel in a special luggage compartment. Then we shopped a little at the Beirut *souqs*, picked up the airline tickets, checked on the hamsters at the university, and visited with our friends there. We saw Amin Kassis and told him about our experiences in Aleppo. We described how his father had so kindly befriended us, as had several other people, such as Mr. Bahhady and Dr. Orita. Amin was delighted to hear about our experiences in his hometown.

That seasonably hot afternoon a swim in the hotel pool felt wonderful. Michael managed to place a call to Dr. Gerald (Jerry) Schneider, his thesis advisor at M.I.T., and told him our return plans. Jerry was pleased to hear that Michael's trip was successful and looked forward to our return.

CHAPTER 20

Awaiting the Flight Home

We had reverse culture shock this time. Beirut was such a cultured and civilized place after our month in Syria. We had dinner at the Pagoda Restaurant with Chinese food served by Lebanese waiters. Awaiting the day of our flight home we explored some nearby sights.

We drove to Baalbek and toured its temple complex of three temples built at the time of Imperial Rome. It was known as Heliopolis (City of the Sun) in Roman times. The temples were dedicated to Jupiter, Venus, and Bacchus. The Temple of Jupiter was completed about 60 CE. Of its original 54 columns only six survive. Eight of them were taken by Justinian to Constantinople to be used in the Hagia Sophia. We admired the six majestic columns remaining.

Michael and Janet in the Temple of Bacchus in Baalbek

Temple of Jupiter remaining columns

The temple of Bacchus was especially well preserved, a large building having 8 columns by 12 columns on a side. There was also an odium, an open-air semi-circular theater for Roman musical performances, which had a lovely view of the sea.

Back at the hotel we swam and enjoyed the sun, played backgammon on our room's tiny balcony using one of the game boards we had purchased in the Aleppo *souq*, and ate dinner at the Olympia Restaurant, which had a three-piece Greek band.

The following day we toured Jaita Grotto, which lies 18 kilometers north of Beirut. It is actually a system of two separate, but interconnected, limestone caves in the Nahr River Valley. The lower grotto can only be visited by boat. The upper grotto, discovered in 1958, had been made accessible to tourists via walkways and a tunnel. The largest known stalactite in the world can be found there. There is evidence that these caves were inhabited by prehistoric man. Perhaps they used stalactites as weapons?

Upon returning to Beirut we had a swim at the hotel and enjoyed a German dinner. Michael expressed his relief that we were on the home stretch.

CHAPTER 21

Returning to Boston

For the trip back to Boston we placed the hamsters carefully in their two traveling cages, each with a piece of apple and some cotton for bedding. We had thirteen animals, so two males shared a compartment. At check-in Michael again inquired about the safety of the baggage compartment for the hamsters. The same as for human passengers, it needed to be pressurized and have oxygen.

We changed planes in Frankfurt, but Michael refused to leave the hamsters unattended, so we did not go into the terminal building.

Michael insures that the hamsters travel safely

It was a good thing he watched over them. The next flight's airplane did not have a pressurized baggage compartment. The authorities decided that the hamster boxes could be placed on edge behind the last seats in the first-class cabin. Therefore, the wild hamsters rode first class, and we rode economy class. Michael was on pins and needles the whole trip back, worrying about his wild hamsters.

When we arrived in Boston our importation papers were found to be in order and the hamsters were put in quarantine at M.I.T. for the required period. Dr. Jerry Schneider met us at the baggage claim. It was the 1970's and Jerry was casually dressed and sported hippy-style long hair, mustache, and goatee. He did not look the part of a dignified professor from M.I.T. In addition, we were returning from the Middle East, where hashish and other drugs could be obtained. Our bags were thoroughly searched, you may be sure!

Eventually the hamsters were placed with the National Institutes of Health in Bethesda, Maryland. They were kept as a separate strain of hamsters, appropriately called the Murphy Strain. They were not allowed to inbreed or to interbreed with other hamster strains. Researchers could request members of this strain for their research.

Mr. Fayek Bahhady came to visit us a year or two later when we lived in Bethesda, Maryland. We were delighted to see him again. We took him to the supermarket, and he was especially amazed to see a whole aisle dedicated to pet food. We recalled that we never saw any pets in Syria. He said he wanted to buy a bar of soap and could not believe the number of brands from which to choose. He finally selected the brand that a TV ad had said was the best. I think his culture shock in our country was as great as our culture shock in his country.

CHAPTER 22

The Legacy of the Expedition

Back home, we housed the dozen wild caught hamsters in individual plastic cages in the vivarium of the Department of Psychology at M.I.T., Cambridge, Massachusetts, where Michael was completing his graduate thesis. These wild animals became exceedingly tame and bred easily in captivity. The first six pregnancies yielded 61 offspring. Despite being observed and disturbed daily, mothers took good care of their young, which is not always true with domestic hamsters.

At this time, my husband was already extremely familiar with the behavior of the domestic hamster (Murphy, 1979). He noted that these wild hamsters seemed indistinguishable from domestic hamsters in appearance. As for behavior, they exhibited all the behaviors that one sees in domestic hamsters. As usual, they scent-marked their cages -- and other hamsters' cages when given the chance. They built beautiful nests, and they hoarded food pellets and placed the food in a pile in one corner of their cage, using another corner as their latrine. The females exhibited normal reproductive, mating, and maternal behavior, and the pups "played" with each other as they matured. Except for mating, or the mother and pups in the nest, individual hamsters were intolerant of each other and attacked and vigorously fought.

The only thing that distinguished the wild hamsters was that every one of them was what Michael called a "Rock Star" hamster, or you might call them the "perfect hamster."

He noted, "All of their natural behaviors were in tune, which is not the case with domestic hamsters purchased from a lab for scientific research. While it is possible to tease some of their natural behaviors out of domestic hamsters, you very infrequently have hamsters as sharp as the ones we captured in the wild" (Murphy, 1971).

After completing his Ph.D. in 1972 my husband, who I will now call Dr. Murphy, accepted a post-doctoral fellowship with the Research Department, National Zoological Park, Smithsonian Institution, in Washington, D.C. He moved a colony of the 1971 wild-caught animals' descendants there, where he studied them in research on evolutionary behavior (Murphy 1973, 1977, 1978, 1980). In 1974, he moved his own colony of wild-caught progeny to the Laboratory of Brain Evolution and Behavior, National Institute of Mental Health, Poolesville, MD, where he maintained the colony and used some of them for research in behavioral neuroscience (Murphy, 1981) and behavioral pharmacology (Murphy, 1980). He disbanded this colony in 1982 when we moved to Texas.

It should be noted that Dr. Murphy began providing progeny of the 1971 wild-caught dozen hamsters to other researchers (e.g., Silvers, Gasser & Murphy, 1975) as soon as the colony was established. After Dr. Murphy left M.I.T., a colony was maintained by Dr. William Nixon, who provided specimens for research on the effects of inbreeding (Ralls, 1982) and immunology (e.g., Streilein and Duncan, 1979). Animals provided to the National Institute of Health (NIH) were used to establish a breeding colony that then provided animals to additional researchers, both at NIH and at other institutions.

Possibly the most significant breakthrough by using the Murphy Strain of hamsters was their role in the discovery of the genetic basis of biological timekeepers. In her review paper, "The chronology of chronobiology, courtesy of hamsters", Madeleine Johnson (2011) wrote:

"Aharoni inbreeding (by necessity) of four wild hamsters in 1930 led an MIT graduate student named Michael Murphy to the frustrated state that all his (lab) hamsters were inbred freaks and to reprise the hamster hunt in 1971." ...

"Had Murphy not worried about inbreeding, there would not be enough diversity to study the time-related genes governing hamster behavior. Murphy's 1971 addition to the hamster breeding stock is what enabled us to clone the tau gene" says neuroscientist Joseph Takahashi of the University of Texas Southwestern, who has studied the genetics of circadian rhythm since the 1980's."

We do not know if anyone still maintains a colony of descendants of the 1971 captured hamsters, but in 1985 the Murphy Strain of hamsters was being maintained at NIH by Andrew Lewis. In 1978 Bill Duncan, Southwestern Medical School, Dallas, Texas, made the historically third capture of live wild hamsters, returning two females to the United States (Murphy, 1985) . Later, in 1997 and 1999, German scientists from the Zoology Department of the University of Halle, assisted by scientists from the University of Aleppo, caught additional specimens of Syrian hamsters near Aleppo and established a breeding colony of these animals at the University of Halle (Gattermann et al., 2001).

* * *

Dr. Michael R. Murphy subsequently had a rewarding career in scientific research and management. Adding physics to his fields of expertise, he often represented his Air Force Research Laboratory, of Brooks Air Force Base, San Antonio, Texas, at international scientific conferences, such as those organized for WHO and NATO, and at other conferences about bioelectromagnetics. I pursued my career in computer systems and databases.

Being recognized as perhaps the world's expert on hamsters, Dr. Murphy was often called upon to facilitate the resurgence of a particular dying strain of hamsters being used in research. Thus, the sixty hamsters we had in our basement in San Antonio!

We continued to enjoy the adventure of international travel and by the time he retired in 2014 we had visited over 60 countries. Dr. Michael R. Murphy passed away in 2018 at the age of 73 having visited a total of 79 countries, a source of pride and happiness for him. He loved exploring the world, and especially meeting and conferring with scientists from other countries. He encouraged proper experiment design and appropriate mathematical analysis of the results. To emphasize this he distributed his large "Show Me the Data" pins, popular at the conferences. He felt that education continues throughout life and that international travel provides a wealth of education to the inquiring mind.

Photos by Michael R. Murphy and Janet E. Murphy

Special thanks to the M.I.T. Psychology Department and Sloan Foundation for partial support of this field trip in 1971.

References and Bibliography

Gattermann, R., Fritzsche, P., Neumann, K., Al-Hussein, I., Kayser, A., Abiad, M. and Yakti, R. (2001) Notes on the current distribution and the ecology of wild golden hamsters (Mesocricetus auratus). Journal of Zoology, 254: 359–365.

Johnson, Madeleine (2011) The chronology of chronobiology, courtesy of hamsters: Biological clockwork still holds secrets. Posted on the website www.science-line.org Life Science section.

Murphy, M. R. (1971) Natural history of the Syrian golden hamster-- a reconnaissance expedition. American Zoology, 11:63.

Murphy, M. R. (1973) Effects of female hamster vaginal discharge on the behavior of male hamsters. Behavioral Biology 9:367 375.

Murphy, M. R. (1977) Interspecific sexual preferences of female hamsters. Journal of Comparative Physiology and Psychology, 91:1337 1346.

Murphy, M. R. (1978) Estrous Turkish hamsters display lordosis toward conspecific males but attack heterospecific males. Animal Behavior, 26:311 312.

Murphy, M. R. (1979) A comprehensive review of hamster behavior. In Inbred and Genetically Defined Strains of Laboratory Animals, Part 2. (Altman, P. L. and Katz, D., eds.) Bethesda, Maryland, Federation of American Societies for Experimental biology, pp 455 465.

Murphy, M. R. (1980) Sexual preferences of male hamsters: Importance of preweaning and adult experience, vaginal secretion, and olfactory or vomeronasal sensation. Behavioral and Neural Biology, 30:323 340.

Murphy, M. R. (1981) Methadone reduces sexual performance and sexual motivation in the male Syrian golden hamster. Pharmacology Biochemistry and Behavior, 14:561 567.

Murphy, M. R., MacLean, P. D., and Hamilton, S. C., (1981) Species typical behavior of hamsters deprived from birth of the neocortex. Science, 213:459 461.

Murphy, M. R. (1985) History of the capture and domestication of the Syrian golden hamster (Mesocricetus auratus Waterhouse) in The Hamster, (Siegel, H. I., ed.) Plenum Publishing Corporation, pp 3-20.

Ralls, Katherine and Ballot, Jonathan (1982) Effect of inbreeding on juvenile mortality in some small mammal Species. Laboratory Animals 16:159-166.

Saouaf, Soubhi, (1965, 3rd edition) Aleppo, Past and Present, English Edition by George F. Miller.

Saouaf, Soubhi, (1957) Six Tours in the Vicinity of Aleppo, English Edition by George F. Miller.

Silvers, W. K., Gasser, D. L., and Murphy, M. R. (1975) Number of histocompatibility loci in Syrian hamsters. Journal of Immunology, 115:1309 1311.

Streilein, J. Wayne and Duncan, William R. (1979) Alloimmune Reactions Among Recently Wild Syrian Hamsters and Classical Inbred Strains Include Antibody Production. Immunogenetics 9:563-573.

Yerganian, G. (1972) History and cytogenetics of hamsters, in Pathology of the Syrian Hamster, Volume 16: Progress in Experimental Tumor Research (F. Homburger, ed.), S. Karger, Basel, pp 2-34.